Global Cities
LONDON

Paul Mason
Photographs by Rob Bowden and Adrian Cooper

Published by
Evans Brothers Limited,
Part of the Evans Publishing Group,
2A Portman Mansions
Chiltern Street
London WIU 6NR

First published 2006
© copyright Evans Brothers Limited

British Library Cataloguing in Publication Data
Mason, Paul, 1967-
London. - (Global cities)
1.London (England) - Juvenile literature
I.Title
942.1'086

ISBN-10: 0237530996
13-digit ISBN (from 1 January 2007) 9780237 530990

Design: Robert Walster, Big Blu Design
Maps and graphics by Martin Darlinson
All photographs are by Rob Bowden (EASI-Images) except:

Adrian Cooper (EASI-Images): 11t, 15t, 17, 19, 20, 21, 23, 24t, 25t, 27, 28b, 29b, 31b, 34t, 35b, 37, 38t, 40t, 42, 43t, 51bl, 51br, 52b, 53, 54b, 55t; Edward Parker (EASI-Images): 16, 18b, 25b; Paul Mason: 43b; Medical Illustration, Great Ormond Street Hospital 29t; Corbis/Bettmann 12b; Corbis 15b

Series concept and project management EASI – Educational Resourcing (info@easi-er.co.uk)

Contents

An urban world

Sometime in 2007 the world's population will, for the first time in history, become more urban than rural. An estimated 3.3 billion people will find themselves living in towns and cities like London, and for many, the experience of urban living will be relatively new. For example, in China, the world's most populous country, the number of people living in urban areas increased from 196 million in 1980 to over 536 million by 2005.

The urban challenge...

This staggering rate of urbanisation (the process by which a country's population becomes concentrated into towns and cities), is being repeated across much of the world and presents the world with a complex set of challenges for the 21st century. Many of these challenges are local, like the provision of clean water for expanding urban populations, but others are global in scale. In 2003 an outbreak of the highly contagious SARS disease demonstrated this as it spread rapidly among the populations of well connected cities across the globe. The pollution generated by urban areas is also a global concern, particularly as urban residents tend to generate more than their rural counterparts.

▼ London in relation to southern England and, inset, its neighbouring countries.

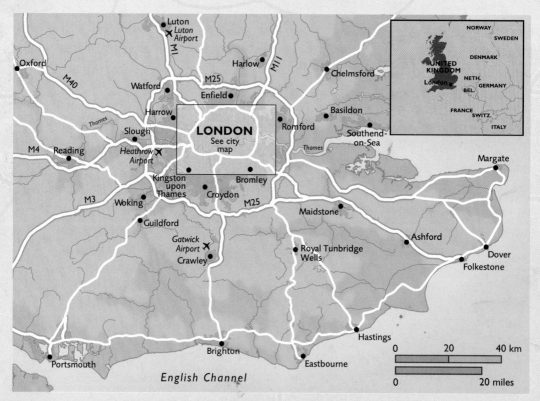

... and opportunity!

Urban centres, and particularly major cities like London, also provide great opportunities for improving life at both a local and global scale. Cities concentrate people and allow for efficient forms of mass transport like subway or light rail networks. Services too, such as waste collection, recycling, education and health can all function more efficiently in a city.

Cities are centres of learning and often the birthplace of new ideas, from innovations in science and technology to new ways of day-to-day living. Cities also provide a platform for the celebration of arts and culture and, as their populations become more multicultural – such celebrations are increasingly global in their reach.

▲ The River Thames winds through the city of London, here passing the financial district.

London facts

Population: Over 7.6 million in 2005

Population density: 4,573 people per square kilometre

Area, Greater London: 1,584 sq km

Parks/green spaces: 147 plus 8 royal parks, 30 per cent of area

Communities: over 50 non-native communities of over 10,000 people

A trading centre

From its very beginnings as a settlement 2,000 years ago, London has been a trading centre. Today it is the richest city in Europe, employing over 3.5 million people – nearly 6 per cent of the entire population of the United Kingdom. People come to London because pay is better than elsewhere in the country (an average of 20 per cent higher) and there are more job opportunities. However living costs are also greater.

A big part of London's success is due to the City of London, which is home to the London Stock Exchange and many globally-important financial institutions. 'The City', as it is known, is part of London but separate from it, governed by its own rules and regulations, and with its own police force. The City's financial influence spreads around the globe: it is the world's biggest centre for international lending, bond trading, and foreign exchange trading.

▼ The famous 'Gherkin' building of the insurance company Swiss Re, one of the financial institutions that have chosen to locate in the City of London.

▼ Central London, with its major roads.

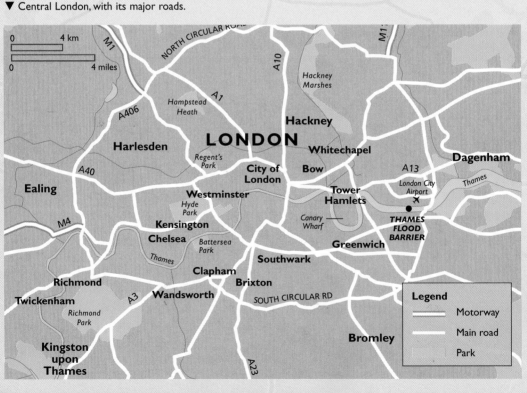

A global melting pot

Many of the world's different nationalities are represented among London's people. People from Commonwealth countries such as Bangladesh, India, Nigeria, South Africa, Jamaica and Australia have all moved to London to live and work. Others have come from elsewhere: there are significant communities of Poles, Turks, Colombians, Argentines and many others.

▶ Members of the long established Bangladeshi community in Brick Lane, one of London's most famous ethnic communities.

Rich and poor

One division in London life is financial, rather than geographical. Areas like Kensington and Chelsea are home to some of the world's richest people, but close by may be social housing for people that may be much less affluent.

▲ New luxury developments in the once working class Docklands are blurring divides within London.

Dividing London

Greater London occupies an area of 1,584 sq km. Londoners cope with the size of their city by mentally dividing it into smaller areas. The first division is north or south of the River Thames: people think of themselves as North or South Londoners. Within these two large areas are many smaller ones, such as Hackney in the north or Brixton in the south. Londoners also think of themselves in terms of east and west. 'Out west' are areas such as Twickenham and Ealing. To the east are the areas where poor manual workers once lived, like Whitechapel and Bow – the homes of 'Cockneys'. A true Cockney is said to be someone born within hearing range of the bells of St Mary Le Bow, a church in the City of London.

The history of London

London began life as a Roman settlement, and at one time was capital of Roman Britain. Despite being abandoned by the Romans in 415, London continued to grow – in 730, the English historian Bede wrote that it was: 'the mart [market] of many nations resorting [travelling] to it by land and sea'. In 1016 London became capital of England. By 1066 King Edward the Confessor had completed the building work on London's famous Westminster Abbey.

Medieval London

Between 1348 and 1375 there were several waves of the 'Black Death' plague, which had already swept across the rest of Europe. In the cramped, unhygienic city, plague spread like wildfire: the disease killed roughly two thirds of the city's population of 75,000 people.

In 1536, King Henry VIII announced the dissolution of the monasteries. Lands and property owned by the Catholic church were sold off. The church had owned many of London's main buildings – these were now sold to private owners, mainly nobles, changing the ownership of the city centre forever.

▲ One of the few medieval buildings remaining in the heart of London.

▼ The plague struck rich and poor, young and old. Houses with dead marked their door with a cross.

▼ The Globe theatre was originally built in 1599. Today, many plays from the 1600s are staged at this reconstructed version.

London first became a truly global city under Elizabeth I. Britain's merchant fleets brought goods to the city, and in 1572 the Royal Exchange was built, where goods from around the world could be traded. Elizabeth's reign was also the time of great playwrights such as William Shakespeare. Today Londoners can spend an evening at the rebuilt Globe Theatre, where many of Shakespeare's plays are now performed, just as they were when they were first written.

Civil war

London played a crucial role in the English Civil War (1642-1649), fought between the supporters of King Charles I and Parliamentary forces demanding greater freedom to make laws. In 1642, Charles had a chance to capture the city but 24,000 Londoners turned out to defend it. Charles withdrew, and missed his chance of victory. He was executed in London's Whitehall almost seven years later, in 1649.

Restoration and the plague

By 1660, Londoners had had enough of the closed theatres and other harsh laws brought in by the ruling Parliamentarians after the Civil War. Londoners welcomed the restoration of the monarchy and the new king, Charles II, with open arms. He repaid them by immediately ordering the theatres to reopen and plays were soon being performed again.

In 1665 the city was again hit by plague. London was, as always, densely packed with people, and that summer's hot weather meant the disease spread quickly. Dogs and cats were thought to carry the plague, so all were killed. Unfortunately this led to an explosion in London's rat population, as there were now no dogs or cats to kill rats. As rats were the true carriers of the fleas that spread the plague to humans, the effect was disastrous, with thousands dying daily.

The Great Fire

The plague died down over winter, but the next year, 1666, Londoners had to deal with an immense fire. On 2 September a fire that started in a baker's caused almost 80 per cent of the city to burn to the ground. The fire leapt from building to building in the narrow streets, and London's old timber-framed houses quickly went up in smoke. Very few people died, but over 100,000 people lost their homes.

In the aftermath of the Great Fire, London was rebuilt to include many of the landmark buildings that are found in the city today. Architects such as Sir Christopher Wren laid out new squares and crescents of houses and rebuilt almost all the city's churches, among them St Paul's Cathedral (right). In just five years 90,000 new homes were built.

The 1700s

Throughout the 1700s, London continued to grow. By now it was the largest city in the world, with a population of almost a million. The growth of the city posed problems for the authorities, as London was rapidly becoming a lawless place. People carried so many weapons that the writer Horace Walpole said people were "forced to travel even at noon as if… going into battle." The problem was only contained when the world's first official police force was founded in 1829.

Meanwhile, trade and industry continued to increase as Britain's empire grew. The docks unloaded increasing amounts of goods from around the world: cotton from India, sugar from Jamaica, wool from Australia, and much else besides. By 1901 there were said to be over seven million people living in London, often crowded into very unhealthy living conditions. Measles, whooping cough, cholera and scarlet fever killed thousands of residents, rich and poor, in the eighteenth and nineteenth centuries.

▲ St Paul's Cathedral is the most famous building in London to arise from the ashes of the Great Fire.

▼ St Katherine Docks – once important for trade in the city has now been converted into dockside homes, shops and restaurants.

Westminster Abbey

Westminster Abbey has played a central role in the history of London and the nation since it was consecrated in 1065. Every monarch since William the Conqueror in 1066, with the exceptions of Edward V and Edward VIII who were never crowned, have had their coronations in the Abbey. It contains the tombs of kings and queens, and the graves and memorials to the great and good of the nation, including statesmen, writers, scientists, artists and musicians – over three thousand people are buried there.

The Abbey was rebuilt in the middle of the thirteenth century when King Henry III (1216-1272) decided to rebuild it in the current Gothic style of architecture. He wanted the Abbey to be not only a place of worship, but also a place for the coronation and burial of monarchs. The Abbey has a large collection of monumental sculpture, including the tomb of the Unknown Warrior.

▲ The west front of Westminster Abbey.

In 1965 the Abbey celebrated its 900th anniversary, with the theme 'One People'. The theme aimed to reflect the Abbey's long involvement with the life of the British people. Today, as well as holding regular services of worship, great events in the life of the nation are marked by special services – such as the funerals of the Princess of Wales and Queen Elizabeth the Queen Mother.

◄ The state funeral of Queen Elizabeth the Queen Mother, in 2002, held in the Abbey.

▲ The first half of the twentieth century saw the building of large suburban areas on the outskirts of the city. Houses with adequate living space for the average family started to become more affordable.

The Twentieth century

As the twentieth century dawned, London was a divided city. The rich lived very well indeed. Britain was the wealthiest country in the world, and London its richest city. Luxury hotels such as the Ritz and expensive department stores such as Harrods grew up at this time.

London's poor still lived in very harsh conditions, though after several strikes by unskilled workers in the late nineteenth century, things were slowly improving. Gas, water, electricity and transport for the city were slowly being brought into public ownership – the London County Council (LCC) had begun to buy up these utilities on behalf of the people of the city. One problem all Londoners still had to contend with was the city's famous 'peasoupers' –

incredibly thick fogs, caused partly by terrible air pollution from nearby factories. After the end of the First World War in 1918, some Londoners began to move to the suburbs. Over the next 20 years they moved to places like Dagenham in the east, one of the LCC's new communities.

The Blitz

During the Second World War (1939–45), the German air force tried to bomb the United Kingdom into submission by attacking London in a series of air raids between September 1940 and May 1941. The raids became known as the 'Blitz', and destroyed large areas of the city. By the end, over 30,000 people had died and 130,000 buildings been destroyed.

Post-war London

By the end of the Second World War, over 80 per cent of London's houses had been damaged in some way by bombing. Partly because of this, more people began to move away from the city, and the population shrank for the first time since the Romans left in 415.

To replace bombed houses, the LCC began a programme of building huge housing estates. To replace departed workers, and those that had died in the war, in the 1950s the government began to recruit workers from Caribbean colonies. People from Trinidad, Jamaica and other islands started to arrive in London for the first time.

During the 1960s the LCC was replaced by the Greater London Council (GLC), which had authority over a much bigger area. By the 1980s the GLC was proposing radical solutions to some of London's problems. These included a subsidised public transport policy, which made buses and trains so cheap that thousands of Londoners stopped using their cars.

The GLC's radical approach was unpopular with the right-wing government of Prime Minister Margaret Thatcher, and in 1986 the GLC was abolished. As a result, until the formation of a Greater London Assembly and the election of a Mayor of London in 2000, the city had no representative government of its own.

▲ During the 1960s, building large tower blocks like this was seen as a good way of providing inexpensive homes for large numbers of Londoners.

◄ Immigrants from Asia and the Caribbean began to arrive in London from the 1950s onwards.

The people of London

London is one of the most ethnically diverse cities in Europe. Over 300 different languages are spoken within the city's boundaries, and it has citizens with family origins from all over the world.

▲ London's many mosques are key meeting places for the city's Muslim communities.

London communities

Londoners from different backgrounds can live in a far more integrated way than people in many other similar cities. Even so, immigrant communities are sometimes associated with particular areas, like the Indian Gujaratis in Wembley, and Afro-Caribbeans in Brixton.

Today over 30 per cent of London's population are either first, second or third-generation immigrants. These are people whose families arrived in London after the Second World War – coming from the Caribbean or the Indian subcontinent. Today, London's new immigrants are more likely to be fleeing the world's wars, and to come from Somalia, Bosnia, Iran or Iraq.

◄ Since 1964, Notting Hill has held a carnival during August. The carnival was originally led by Trinidadian immigrants, but today is a multicultural event.

Juliano and Talita

Brazilians Juliano and Talita share a one-bed flat with another couple and their young daughter in Harlesden, a part of London with a growing community of Brazilians and Portuguese. In London Juliano works as a motorcycle courier, despite having trained to be a pharmacist in Brazil. Talita works as a cleaner – at university she studied sports science. Juliano has an Italian father, which means he can have an Italian passport. As Italy is part of the European Union, Juliano can work in the UK.

Juliano first came to the UK in 1999 to earn money to pay for university. He worked as a barman, hotel cleaner, and various other odd jobs. He returned to Brazil and studied for his pharmacy degree for four years. He met Talita in Brazil, at university. After graduation they came back to London together. Juliano says, "I told Talita, I know every place, trust me... but after six months I thought it was a complete mistake. Everything seemed to go wrong. My motorcycle broke, then it got stolen, all in my first week of work. I almost wanted to go back. Talita said to me 'Let's stay, we made the effort to come here.'"

Juliano could adapt his Brazilian degree and get work in a pharmacy in London, but it is difficult, with little English and a loose grasp of how the city works, to find out how to go about doing this. He relies on word-of-mouth among fellow Brazilians more than anything. There's also hardly enough time to find out because his job takes up too much of his time.

Some immigrants to London have made a shorter, less perilous journey to reach the city. These are people drawn to the city by its facilities, good wages and other attractions. They come from all over Britain and Europe, particularly the new member states of the European Union.

Alongside the immigrant communities are 'native' Londoners: those whose grandparents and parents weren't tempted to move out to the suburbs.

▶ London population movements 1950-2015. The city's population level is not expected to fluctuate in the forseeable future.

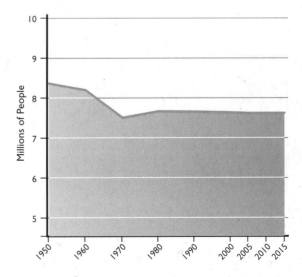

▲ London's large population creates huge amounts of waste daily.

Population issues

London is one of Europe's largest cities – in 2005 only Paris and Moscow had bigger populations. With a population of well over seven million, London has more inhabitants than many countries, including Israel, Denmark, and Norway.

In 1950 London was the third-largest city in the world; but by 2015, it will no longer even make the top 30, as other cities of global importance continue to expand in population. In addition to this change, over the last 50 years London's population has slowly been shrinking. Even the large numbers of new citizens arriving from abroad and elsewhere in the UK cannot keep pace with the numbers of people leaving.

In recent years the trend of people leaving the city has been accelerated by the increase in property values. Many Londoners – like a large proportion of British people generally – own their own homes. Someone who bought a house for £100,000 in 1980 might find it worth over £1 million today. As property prices are lower outside the capital, some Londoners have left, using the money they made to start a new life elsewhere.

▶ London's roads are always busy, especially so when people are trying to get to or from work, or leaving the city for the weekend.

A crowded city

Today London's population is stable at around 7.6 million people, who live in an area of 1,584 sq km. As 30 per cent of London is made up of parks and green space, the area actually available for housing and businesses is far smaller than this. Londoners are used to being jammed into tight spaces: in queues, on pavements, and travelling on the city's underground 'Tube' trains, for example.

The size of London's population raises a wide variety of challenges for the city's planners. Many Londoners are living inside the boundaries of a city originally laid out to fit far fewer people, moving more slowly. The city's infrastructure (for example the roads, transport network, power and water supplies, and the other things that make it possible to live in a modern city) dates originally from well over 100 years ago.

▲ During the morning and evening rush hour public transport, like the Tube shown here, can be very crowded.

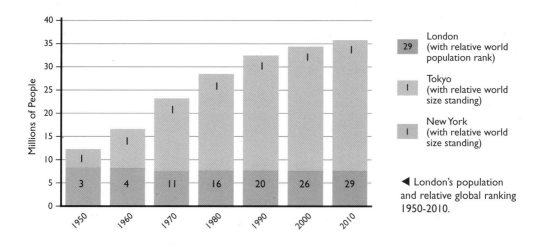

London (with relative world population rank) 29

Tokyo (with relative world size standing) 1

New York (with relative world size standing) 1

◄ London's population and relative global ranking 1950-2010.

Pressures

Today, a Londoner from 1900 would find the layout of central London familiar. The biggest difference would be that cars, buses, bicycles and motorbikes use the familiar streets of Victorian London, rather than horse-drawn carriages. Each day millions of pollution-creating cars and other vehicles take to the city's roads.

Other issues are less visible, but no less important: the same Victorian sewer system now carries the waste of millions: from toilets, washing machines, dish-washers, showers and other modern appliances; tonnes of litter and other waste have to be disposed of every day; power and water have to be supplied to millions of homes and businesses; housing, schools and hospitals are all needed. All these issues are crucial if the city is to be a viable place for people to live in the future.

▲ Concern about crime is one of the things people dislike about living in London. London's police force, the Metropolitan Police, tries to be highly visible as a way of reassuring people.

Conflicts and crime

Racial and cultural conflicts are not new in London, though historically Londoners have been more likely to stage a riot against the authorities than against other Londoners, wherever they are from. Nonetheless, conflicts between different ethnic groups of Londoners exist. In some parts of London political parties have fanned the flames of these conflicts as a way of winning votes. Crime is a concern for Londoners, with muggings and burglaries at the top of the list. Often these are linked to other problems like alcohol and drug abuse. People with no job or money pay for their addictions by breaking into houses and flats, to steal goods that are then sold for a fraction of their true cost.

Language challenge

London has large numbers of first-generation immigrants for whom English is not a first language. The government is keen for new citizens to adapt to British values, and the first step for many immigrant children is to learn English. In some London schools there are more Punjabi speakers, for example, than English speakers.

Homelessness

Homelessness is a problem in London, with whole communities of people living on the streets, under bridges or in abandoned buildings. Some have come to the city from elsewhere in the hope of a good life, and instead found it impossible to get a place to live or a job. Among the homeless are also people with mental health problems, runaways, alcoholics and drug addicts.

◀ This man is selling the *Big Issue*, a weekly paper sold by homeless people as a way of earning money.

CASE STUDY

Edwin, Crisis volunteer

Born in 1944, Edwin came to London as a soldier in the Royal Scots Dragoon Guards. In 1972 he had a number one hit single, 'Amazing Grace', with his regimental band. At the same time he started drinking heavily. He was thrown out of the army: 34 years of homelessness and substance abuse followed.

In 2005 he moved into a home, in Uxbridge. "I had a dream of a Rolls Royce and golden streets, but it wasn't to be. There was no gold." He no longer drinks and has become a volunteer for Crisis, a charity that helps homeless people improve their lives, giving art and craft classes. He also gives advice to young homeless people. "When you're on the streets you see all walks of life. People's marriages break down, people lose their jobs, mental health, bankruptcy ... there's all sorts of reasons why people are on street corners. Main thing is we're all human beings. You have to fend for yourself and keep your head looking out, watching your back all the time. I'm one of two survivors out of a group of 15 people I used to hang around with. The rest have died from alcohol. London has changed. There are more young people on the streets. More fighting, too. It's more dangerous now than 20 years ago. Street people are stealing and robbing from one another, and that never used to happen. They can't trust each other. Now I come home and put on some CDs, do some cooking. It's hard to get used to paying the rent on time, buying food for yourself, and cooking. But, of course, it's worth it."

Living in the city

Perhaps the most pressing problem London faces is creating enough affordable housing. Housing costs have risen steeply over the last 50 years. As wages have risen in the better-paid industries like banking or law, house prices and rents have risen as well. This has meant that workers in essential services, like nursing, cannot afford homes.

Types of housing

London contains a wide variety of different types of housing. In the centre, where space is precious, most homes are flats or apartments, often created by dividing up large old houses. Further from the middle of the city, houses become more common. Further out still, people's houses might even be semi-detached, with a garage and garden. The city's public housing is scattered throughout London, known as 'council estates' or just 'estates'. Many of these are high-rise blocks of flats, originally designed to house low-paid workers. People are able to rent these homes from the local government for an affordable rent, provided that there are enough free homes. In the 1980s the national government introduced laws that allowed people to buy their

▲ In recent years, many older buildings have been demolished to make way for new homes.

rented council homes at low prices. Many took advantage of the offer, and today some of this accommodation is privately owned, and unavailable for poorer residents.

▼ Historic properties with character, like these Georgian period houses in north London, can sell for very high prices.

Essential workers

Few of the essential workers, such as nurses, teachers, firefighters and ambulance drivers, earn enough to buy a home. To provide them with housing, housing associations may offer them an affordable way to own a share in a property. The worker buys a part share, then pays reduced rent to the association for the other share. The London Assembly is trying to make sure that when new housing schemes are built, some of the homes are made available to these essential workers so that they can live near their work.

▶ Some of London's newly built homes are set aside for 'key' or 'essential' workers – teachers and nurses, for example.

Parks and gardens

Parks and gardens take up almost a third of London. These green spaces are important to Londoners, who put them to a wide variety of uses. On Hampstead Heath, for example, are the famous Bathing Ponds, real ponds used as swimming pools. People use the parks for exercise, including running, football, horse riding, and for leisure activities like picnics. They're also important as an escape from the hustle of city life, for breathing a bit of fresh air and relaxing.

▼ Enjoying St James's Park, one of the large parks in the centre of the city.

▼ Average temperatures and rainfall for London.

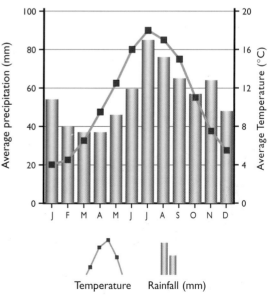

Temperature   Rainfall (mm)

▲ High-fashion stores are found in areas such as Old Bond Street, Covent Garden, and Knightsbridge.

Shopping

London is famous as a centre for fashion designers. In Covent Garden and on Old Bond Street the shops contain clothes from designers such as Paul Smith, Stella McCartney and Alexander McQueen. Most Londoners buy their clothes at the less expensive shops that are found everywhere in the city. Clothes are also an important part of the city's outdoor markets, where everything from a new pair of socks to an antique ball-gown can be bought.

Food

Each area of London once had at least a weekly food market, and many were held every day. Since the Second World War may of these markets have closed due to competition from supermarkets, but in several parts of London they remain a thriving part of the community.

   Among the most famous are London's traditional old wholesale markets, such as the Smithfield meat market, which has been in existence since 1327. Produce from the countryside arrived at Smithfield, to be sold

on to the butchers, greengrocers, stallholders, flower sellers and chefs of the city. Farmers' markets are increasingly popular in London. In these, small-scale food producers bring their goods to the city to sell them direct to the people who will eat them. Many farmers' markets sell organic goods, which are becoming more popular every year.

▶ These butchers work at Smithfield meat market.

Maggy O'Grady

Maggy shops at the farmers' market in Peckham Square. Maggy, a Camberwell resident of 25 years, is here to buy fresh bread. Last week she bought Turk's head (a vegetable) and squashes. "As autumn and winter set in, it's about keeping the summer sunshine in my kitchen. It's more expensive to buy from farmers' markets, but I think it's worth it. Of course it's about not going to a supermarket, but it isn't just about the food. Damilola Taylor, a young boy, was murdered near here a few years ago, and for our community spirit it is important to participate in things like local markets. It helps keep the area lively. You could say it helps dispel ghosts."

▲ London has some of the oldest markets in the world; today they are increasing in popularity once more.

Urban health issues

Londoners are faced with several challenges if they are to remain fit and healthy while living in the city. Many Londoners get up by 7.00 a.m. to have breakfast and head off to work, taking an hour or more to arrive. They have a busy, long day, and get home late in the evening. They may not have the time or energy to cook a meal from individual ingredients. Instead they rely on convenience foods, which simply have to be heated up, or fast foods, which are collected ready-cooked and eaten.

These foods have greatly increased in popularity since the 1980s, when they first appeared. Unfortunately, they are now linked to a number of serious health problems, including heart problems and obesity. Many children in particular are now suffering health problems as a result of eating too much convenience and fast food. In 2005, a local TV chef, Jamie Oliver, helped to raise awareness about healthy eating during a campaign to persuade schools in London (and nationally) to

▲ Joggers are a common sight on the streets.

▼ The importance of healthy eating is now emphasised in schools.

Just Eat More
(fruit & veg)

CARROTS

provide more nutritious meals. Another issue for London is the amount of alcohol consumed by its residents. With so many restaurants, bars, theatres and pubs, many people find that their social lives can very easily involve drinking alcohol. Alcohol is responsible for increased levels of heart disease and liver problems, among many other health problems.

The city's air pollution also causes health problems. An increasing proportion of children are suffering from the breathing difficulty asthma, which is a potential killer. Some experts have linked this increase to increased air pollution from cars.

Hospitals and doctors

Like people in the rest of the UK, Londoners can use the free National Health Service. Few other cities of global importance are in countries with a similar health service. Anyone who is sick or injured can visit a doctor's surgery or hospital without having to pay. There is a standard fee for prescribed medicines, but people with long term illnesses, such as diabetes, do not have to pay. There are also private hospitals and clinics, many in the area around Harley Street in Marylebone.

The city's healthcare system is not without its problems, however. Finding enough well-trained staff is always a problem. Stress, high-living costs, and a better standard of living elsewhere mean staff can be hard to hold on to. Many staff are recruited from other countries, where the rates of pay may be worse than in London, or the living conditions worse. Late at night, Accident and Emergency Departments can sometimes be alarming places, as those who have drunk too much and hurt themselves mix with other patients.

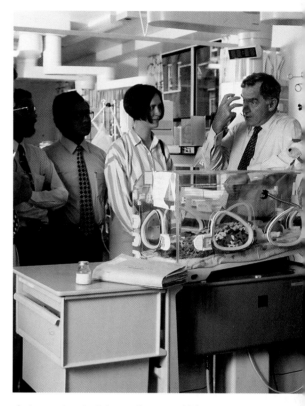

▲ Among London's hospitals are world-famous teaching hospitals such as Great Ormond Street Hospital for Children, where paediatricians can learn new skills.

▶ Health workers at a health fair, held as part of an NHS outreach programme in Southwark.

The London economy

London has an economy that contributes over US$100 billion to the UK economy. The banking and financial sector is the largest contributor to the city's economy. Other important industries include the media (television and radio companies, newspapers and publishers), a very large retail sector and the large law firms based in the City of London.

There is little manufacturing industry, so most Londoners work in the service sector, including the large public sector — such as the national or local government departments, of which there are many based in central London. A few workers in the financial sector can earn huge salaries, but most London workers find life less financially rewarding. Inner London is the wealthiest part of the United Kingdom, with a resilient economy that can withstand changes in economic outlook, but despite that there still remains some unemployment, ranging from almost zero in the City, to 13 per cent in Tower Hamlets, just a ten minute walk from the City. The high cost of travelling to work, plus higher food prices and more expensive accommodation than the rest of the country, mean that some people end up struggling to make ends meet. Worst off of all are the people who work in the city centre at unskilled jobs such as street sweeping or office cleaning. These jobs are low paid, but the basic costs of living in the city are similar to everyone else's.

▼ Getting ready for the lunch rush at Leadenhall Market. Jobs like waiting on tables, cleaning and kitchen work are often poorly paid and done by recent immigrants.

Creative industries

The multiple branches of the creative and media industries are an important part of the city economy – they provide over 400,000 jobs in London. The city also provides the infrastructure-related jobs that all big cities have such as the transport and construction industries and road and sewer maintenance. There are some small manufacturing businesses, and an enormous retail sector.

▲ News photographers waiting outside the Houses of Parliament. The national news media is based in London and is a major employer.

CASE STUDY

Ndidi Ekubia – silversmith

Originally from Manchester, Ndidi Ekubia is a silversmith. A traditional trade, silversmithing has recently been revived and celebrated by organisations like the Craft Council and the Jerwood Prize. Cockpit Arts, where Ndidi has worked for the last three years, is a charity that provides affordable studio space in Holborn and Deptford for designers and makers. They have an award scheme, called the Seedbed Award, which gives discounted rents to individuals and businesses that are just starting out.

"I work very long hours, and have to support myself with a second job at the moment. Without organisations like Cockpit it would be more difficult for designers and makers like me to survive. I work here because it's affordable, and also because I'm surrounded by other designer-makers. Silversmithing makes a lot of noise, so I need to be in the kind of environment where it is acceptable to do this kind of work. It's difficult to find affordable space like this in London. And what's good about Cockpit is they also give you business support and help with publicity and financial advice. There is also 'Open Studios' twice a year: everybody here exhibits their work and hundreds of people from all over London come and buy our work."

The City

At the heart of London – literally and metaphorically – is the City. Physically, the City is made up of the area governed by the Corporation of London, which is the oldest local authority in England. The financial institutions that together comprise the City make it one of the most powerful financial organisations in the world. The City is sometimes called the 'Square Mile', because of the compact size of its core area. Despite its tiny size, the City contributes about three per cent of the UK's GDP and about 13 per cent of London's GDP. A few facts underline the sheer amount of money that the City generates: US$504 billion of foreign exchange turnover passes through the City every day; 70 per cent of all Eurobonds are

▲ The Lloyds Building, home to one of the world's biggest insurance companies, Lloyds of London.

▼ The London Metal Exchange, which helps regulate the world's trade in metals.

LONDON METAL EXCHANGE

traded in London; US$2,000 billion of metal stock is traded each year in the City; and US$884 billion is traded on the international futures market every day. In 2005, 287 foreign companies were listed on the London Stock Exchange, where shares in companies are bought and sold. Many of the UK companies listed on the exchange also trade or own manufacturing facilities around the world.

The Corporation of London

The Corporation of London provides the City with its infrastructure, and runs the City of London Police (a separate force from the Metropolitan Police, who are in charge of the rest of London). The Corporation also maintains 4,047 hectares of open space in and around London, including Epping Forest and Hampstead Heath. It runs three big food markets (Smithfield, Billingsgate and Spitalfields), and provides affordable residential housing across London. The Corporation can do this because of the City's wealth, and with rent from its large landholdings.

Chris Giles

Chris is the Economics Editor for *The Financial Times* (or FT), a financial newspaper that began as a tip sheet and has been the most important business newspaper in London and the world for over 100 years. Like many businesses, the FT feels it is important to keep an office in the City. "Computers mean that trading and deals can be done almost anywhere now," explains Chris, "but it is still important to be in the City. All the big global banks have an office in London and many large companies too." London's history as a financial centre began with its trading past and the square mile, 'the City', was the focus for raising funds and buying and selling commodities. Chris explains that the financial sector has spread to new areas of London, such as the Docklands and the West End, where some

smaller companies have located. "The financial sector has been growing very rapidly for the past 10 years, much faster than other parts of the UK economy. I can see no slow-down in this growth and London is still the most important place to be for business."

The Livery

The Livery is the name for a group of 107 livery guilds based in the City. These are ancient trade associations, such as the Goldsmith's Company. Many are still important to the trade they are named after, for example the Goldsmith's Company is responsible for testing precious metals for their purity. In 1478 the Company passed a rule that all precious metals had to be brought to its hall to be marked with the correct purity. This is the origin of the word 'hallmark', meaning a mark that reveals the purity of a metal.

▶ London's Guildhall was the original home of the City's many livery guilds.

Industrial decline

After the Second World War, London's traditional industrial sites slowly became run down. Manufacturing in the UK in general had begun to decline, as the economy shifted towards a service industry base. At the same time the importance of London as a port decreased. The East End docks, which had provided employment for generations of Londoners, fell into disuse. They became abandoned and derelict – the largest inner city 'brownfield' site in Europe.

▲ Some areas of London are still home to derelict buildings once used for businesses or industry.

Redevelopment

In recent years many of London's run down and derelict areas have been redeveloped, sometimes with the help of the UK government. The area around Greenwich was chosen as the site of the Millennium Dome, a giant 'attraction' that cost about £840 million and has yet to find a permanent use. More successfully, the Canary Wharf area was redeveloped into offices and homes on a formerly derelict site. Many businesses, particularly financial institutions, relocated to the Canary Wharf area, attracted by lower rents and new transport links.

▼ The East End around Canary Wharf in Docklands has become a rival location to the City for global corporations.

The 2012 Olympics

London's winning bid to host the 2012 Olympics will allow the regeneration of run-down areas of the city. The transport links and sports facilities that the Olympics will need will later be available for London's citizens, so improving their lives. Other cities, notably Barcelona in Spain, have used the Olympics in just this way.

◀ Signs celebrate the fact that London hosts the Olympics in 2012.

CASE STUDY

Rufus Clarke

Rufus is a Neighbourhood Youth Co-ordinator, aged 45. He's lived in Tower Hamlets all his life, and been a youth worker for 15 years. "My work is about young people's futures. Tonight, for example, I've got a social enterprise project running which trains them how to build computers. And once they have built one, and pass the course with the right skills, they keep the computer. It's an incentive for them to get skills. Another example is a youth banking scheme where money the council would pay for things like graffiti removal and community work, like painting old people's homes, they pay into an account for young people. When the young people have earned credits through doing the community work they can go out and buy things. Because of the 2012 Olympics money is likely to come to the area, directly and indirectly, so I'm encouraging the young people I work with to get some sort of skill before the Olympics come. I don't want to see young people left by the wayside. The building of Canary Wharf didn't do much for our community – the homes were too expensive for the younger generation to afford. I hope the facilities built during the Olympics will be available and accessible to all our community."

Managing London

London has been the home of first England's, and then the UK's, national government since the eleventh century. The UK Government is centred on the Houses of Parliament at Westminster. London is governed by an elected Mayor and the London Assembly, based at County Hall across the Thames from the Tower of London.

▲ The Houses of Parliament are home to the UK's national government.

The Mayor

The first city-wide Mayor was elected in 2000, with elections subsequently held every four years. In 2000 and 2004, Ken Livingstone was elected, partly because Londoners remembered his time in charge of the Greater London Council during the 1980s. The Mayor works with the borough councils (see p. 37-38), plus the transport, police, fire and development authorities, to develop London-wide policies including reducing crime; improving public transport; reducing traffic congestion; making more affordable housing available; improving deprived areas and the environment; supporting tourism and economic development; and planning for London's future. The City of London has its own mayor – The Lord Mayor of London, whose role involves representing the Corporation of London, and promoting the City abroad.

The Assembly

The Mayor is more powerful than the Assembly; the Assembly's main role is to act as a check for the Mayor's activities. The Assembly has to have a two-thirds majority of its twenty five members to overturn one of the Mayor's policies. The Mayor's office and the London Assembly are funded in various ways. Some money comes from a share of the council tax paid to local governments by everyone who lives or has a business in the city. Most money comes as grants from the UK government.

▼ The new, futuristic City Hall, seen here with Tower Bridge in the background, is home to the Mayor's office and the London Assembly. City Hall, which opened in 2002, sits by the Thames, across the river from the Tower of London.

Voting in London

To vote in city elections voters must be living in London, be a UK, EU or Commonwealth resident, aged 18 or over, and registered to vote. Voters in mayoral elections can place two votes, a first-choice and a second-choice. If no one wins the election when all the first-choice votes have been counted, only the two candidates with the highest numbers of votes remain in the contest. The second-choice votes of everyone who voted for other candidates are then counted, to see which of the two remaining candidates they prefer. In this way, the winner is decided. For the Assembly, voters also have two votes. One elects a named candidate for the local area; the other goes towards a party or candidate from a city-wide list.

► Town halls are where the administrative units of smaller areas of London are based.

Local government

As well as having a Mayor and the London Assembly, Londoners are represented on their 32 borough councils, which act for the city's boroughs or districts.

These are responsible for such things as refuse collection, schools, road maintenance and street lighting in their particular areas of the city. The borough councils work with the Mayor and Assembly. For example, if the Mayor develops a plan for a London-wide recycling scheme, the boroughs are the bodies that actually have to put the scheme into action.

Local action

History shows that Londoners have a tradition of direct action if there is something that they aren't happy about. Some Londoners, aware of the city's problems, are not content to wait for the Mayor to put a strategy together, then for their borough council to act on the strategy. Instead they take matters into their own hands. Sometimes they start campaigns, for example petitioning for an improvement in the standard of school dinners, or to save a local sports field from being turned into a housing estate. On other occasions they actually get together and work on schemes to improve their city. Volunteering for this sort of campaign is becoming more widespread as people see the success of other schemes.

► This was a special collection to collect waste that had been illegally dumped and then collected together by volunteers. The local council worked with them to collect and dispose of it – an example of cooperation between city and residents.

Fishing the Wandle

The River Wandle runs for nine miles, from Croydon and Carshalton in the south to the Thames in the north. The river has a strong flow, making it perfect for water-powered factories: at one time there were nearly 100 mills along the banks. Unfortunately these mills dumped their waste into the river, and it became badly polluted. Local campaigner Alan Suttee (right) remembers that, "In the late 1960s the Wandle was officially designated an open sewer. And in the 70s I remember it running red, pink, or blue, depending on what dye they were using in the local tanneries."

In the 1990s a small team of local residents, led by Suttee, began to work on clearing the river of debris, as long sections had become choked with weeds and rubbish. "We've pulled out supermarket trolleys, motorbikes, safes, and even guns. You wouldn't believe what's in that river," said Suttee.

Many of the volunteers were fishermen who knew that the river had once been famous for its trout fishing. They were first rewarded in 2002 when a fly fisherman caught a one-kilogramme brown trout on the river. It is believed to be the first trout caught in London in 70 years.

◀ A volunteer removes rubbish from the river.

Transport in London

London was home to the world's first underground train system which opened in 1863. London also has a local system of overland trains. Today over three million passengers use the underground system (or 'tube' as it is known) every weekday. The network has over 500 trains and employs more than 12,000 people. The tube has been expanded greatly from the early days, and this growth is continuing today with work on extending the Jubilee line.

Complementing the tube system are London's buses. In the past these were criticised for being slow and unreliable. Increased bus use is a key goal for those in charge of transport for London. To encourage this, more buses have been introduced to improve service frequency and bus lanes created to reduce the

▲ New buses using more eco-friendly fuels are being introduced.

problem of buses being held up by congestion; cameras record car drivers who use bus lanes and issue them with fines. In late 2005, free bus travel for under-16s in full-time education was introduced as a further incentive. These policies have contributed to a 38 per cent increase in bus use between 2000 and 2005 and there are today over 6,800 buses carrying an estimated six million people every weekday.

▲ ▶ Every day, millions of people use the Underground to get around. There are stations dotted everywhere, making it a convenient way of crossing the city.

▲ The M25 is the world's largest ring road, completely circling London. Delays are often so bad that people joke it's the world's largest car park!

External transport links

London is linked into a system of eight motorways, and once drivers have escaped the London traffic they can head in any direction they choose. London is ringed by the M25 motorway, which feeds on to routes in all directions.

London is also well connected to other UK cities (and even some in mainland Europe) through an extensive train network. Engineering work on a high-speed train link from the centre of London to the Channel Tunnel and Europe is expected to finish in 2007. The link is a 108 km line, with much of the London section passing through deep tunnels. A 3 km stretch will pass under the Thames at Dartford, then a 19 km tunnel will lead to St Pancras station

▲ Eurostar trains go from central London to Paris and Brussels.

in central London. London is served by four international airports – City, Heathrow, Gatwick and Stansted, though the last two are actually outside Greater London. London's role as a sea port has declined, nonetheless, ships still bring goods to the city from around the world. Most of the sea-borne goods destined for London arrive at Tilbury, 30 km to the east of the city.

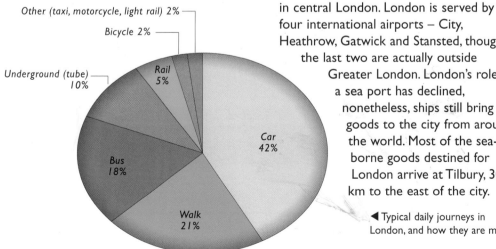

Other (taxi, motorcycle, light rail) 2%

Bicycle 2%

Underground (tube) 10%

Rail 5%

Car 42%

Bus 18%

Walk 21%

◀ Typical daily journeys in London, and how they are made.

Traffic congestion

Even though the narrow old street plan of central London was not laid out with cars in mind, they still need to find a route through the city. In the past the volume of traffic caused terrible congestion, with whole areas of the city 'gridlocked' by lines of traffic at the busiest times of day.

One of the Mayor's main priorities has been to try to ease this congestion, which pollutes the centre of the city and causes health problems for London's citizens. Congestion has been tackled in two main ways. The first is through 'congestion charging' – see p. 44. The second is by encouraging people to use alternative forms of transport.

Cycling and walking

The city is trying to encourage more people to cycle in London, because of the health and environmental benefits cycling brings. Courier companies that need to move packages around the city quickly have found using cyclists as quick or quicker than motorbikes. This emphasis is in contrast with large numbers of still developing cities which may have terrible pollution problems, yet see thousands of people abandoning their bikes for cars. In London, cycle traffic increased by 67 per cent between 2000 and 2005. The number of cyclists was still very small, though, at just 101,000 people using bicycles as their main mode of transport. Many people are put off cycling by the idea of riding in the aggressive London traffic, which carries a risk of injury.

London is also trying to make it easier for people to walk around the city. Pedestrian routes have been improved, road crossings have been added, and signposts on pavements give people directions around central London.

▶ Increasing numbers of bicycle lanes have been created, in the hope that more Londoners will get on their bikes.

▲ London's streets still suffer bad congestion, even after the introduction of the Congestion Charge.

▶ Small fold-up bikes like this man's make it easy to use a combination of trains, buses and bike.

▼ The use of bicycles leapt after terrorists attacked London's Underground system in July 2005.

CASE STUDY

Sarah Hanratty, cyclist

"It always used to take me at least an hour to get to work with a Tube journey across London," says Sarah Hanratty. Sarah used to leave home at about 7.30 am in the morning. "One day I decided to cycle. I really felt like riding, but was worried about how long it would take. So I set off at 7.00 am. I figured the bike would take at least twice as long as the Tube." A surprise was in store: "I actually got to work at 7.30 am. It had taken me half an hour. After that, I never went on the Tube again."

The congestion charge

In 2002, London was one of the first of the world's major cities to announce the introduction of congestion charging. This means charging drivers for entering the busy centre of the city. The aim was to discourage unnecessary journeys, reduce the traffic flow, and increase revenue for the city's government. At the same time as the charge was introduced, the Mayor's office increased the number of city buses, encouraging people to use public transport rather than their cars.

Transport for London, the body in overall charge of transport in the city, put forward three main reasons for the charge being introduced:
• London had the worst traffic congestion in the UK, and among the worst in Europe.
• Drivers in central London spent 50 per cent of their time in queues.
• Every weekday morning, the equivalent of 25 busy motorway lanes of traffic tried to enter central London.

It was estimated that lost time caused by congestion cost businesses £2–4 million (US$3.5-7 million) every week.

The charging scheme works between 7.00 a.m. and 6.30 p.m. from Monday to Friday. With a few exceptions, anyone driving in central London during that time has to pay. At first the cost was £5.00, which in 2005 increased to £8.00. Drivers can pay on-line, by phone, or by text message. Cameras photograph vehicles entering the charging area, record their number plates and check whether they have paid or not. If not, the computer sends out notice of a fine.

Congestion charging has its critics. People claim that it has had a knock-on effect on traffic outside the charging zone, which has become busier with people parking there to avoid the charge. As a result, many areas outside the charging zone have introduced 'resident parking' schemes, where local people pay for a

▼ Signs painted on the road warn drivers they are entering the congestion-charging zone.

▲ The Congestion Charge zone is clearly marked.

permit to park their cars. Anyone without a permit cannot park during the day.

Small businesses based inside the congestion charging zone have complained bitterly about the effect the charge has had on their businesses, especially if quick deliveries are required. Florists, fish-mongers and butchers, or any business that needs to deliver fresh produce have had to suffer a large increase in their business' running costs. Many small businesses that have ceased trading since the introduction of the charge have blamed their failure on its costs.

The increase in the number of buses has also been controversial, as the investment in new buses has been expensive. Many critics have complained that the money spent on the buses is wasted – they are mainly empty outside the rush hour, and over-full during them.

In 2007 the charging zone will be extended west to include the boroughs of Kensington and Chelsea. This proposal has been unpopular with local residents. They argue the original central congestion charging zone was a less residential area, and they are being unfairly targeted.

Culture, leisure and tourism

London has the greatest concentration of major attractions in Britain. These include four World Heritage Sites – The Palace of Westminster, The Tower of London, Maritime Greenwich and Kew Gardens – and 238 attractions that are free to enter. London's tourist bosses boast: "There is nowhere else in the world where you can see so much for so little." London's top visitor attractions range from ancient to modern. These, plus the theatres, restaurants, pubs and clubs of the city, bring billions of tourist pounds each year to the city. Visitors come from all over the UK and the rest of the world.

▲ A military band marches past the front of Buckingham Palace, the Queen's London home.

The National Gallery

The National Gallery faces Trafalgar Square, and is the most popular visitor attraction in the whole city. As with many museums and galleries, entry is free. The National is home to one of the world's greatest collections of Western European art, including works by great artists such as Botticelli, Turner, Cezanne and Van Gogh. The separate National Portrait Gallery is at the back of the National, and houses pictures of famous and infamous people from Britain's past and present.

▶ Nelson's Column, in Trafalgar Square, with the National Gallery in the background. Trafalgar Square is a popular place for New Year's celebrations and political demonstrations.

Tate Modern

Tate Modern is the UK's national museum of modern art. It makes quite a contrast to the National – instead of being housed in a grand old building, the Tate Modern is in a converted power station beside the River Thames. As well as established artists, the gallery includes exhibitions by new artists. Its cavernous main vault has shown some giant pieces of work, which have gone on to be shown around the world.

▲ The Tate Modern can be reached by footbridge from the north bank of the Thames. The bridge was opened as part of London's millennium celebrations.

▼ The London Eye – the big wheel is on the south bank of the Thames. It gives views across the whole of London.

The London Eye

Conceived as an entry in a millennium landmark competition (which it didn't win), the London Eye is now one of the city's visitor attractions. Taller than the Statue of Liberty in New York, or Big Ben in London, the Eye is a giant wheel providing views of London. On a clear day, views from the Eye can stretch as far as Windsor Castle, almost 40 km away. Visitors are carried in one of the Eye's 32 capsules, which have mainly glass walls: when fully used, the wheel can carry 15,000 people a day.

London's top ten tourist attractions

This list is based on the number of visitors per year:
1 National Gallery
2 British Museum
3 Tate Modern art gallery
4 London Eye
5 Natural History Museum
6 Science Museum
7 Tower of London
8 Victoria and Albert Museum
9 National Portrait Gallery
10 National Maritime Museum

The value of tourism

Tourists from overseas are crucial to the city's economy. These visitors fall into two broad camps. First are visitors to the UK who pass through London on their way elsewhere – 50 per cent of visitors to the UK spend time in London. Second are people who come specifically to see the city, who tend to be there longer.

The financial value of tourism is huge: the industry directly and indirectly brings in approximately £15 billion (US$26 billion) per year, or 10 per cent of the city's GDP. The benefits of tourism are not only financial, they are also cultural: tourist income helps to pay for many of the city's historical attractions, museums and galleries. Overseas visitors buy 30 per cent of all theatre tickets and make up 50 per cent of those going to sites such as the Tower of London. Without them, many attractions would struggle to survive, and would not be available for Londoners themselves to enjoy.

Tourism to London is affected by events around the world. Since 2001, fears about terrorism, SARS and bird flu have had a negative impact on visitor numbers. Economic depression in Japan has meant fewer wealthy visitors from the Far East, and a fall in the value of both the US dollar and the European euro against the UK pound makes it harder for visitors from abroad to afford to come to London.

The Olympics of 2012 are expected to boost the number of visitors. As soon as the decision that the Games were coming to London was announced, preparations for the sports stadiums, transport facilities and accommodation began. Over 10,000 competitors, their coaches, hundreds of thousands of spectators, television crews, reporters and others will give a huge, but temporary, boost to London's economy.

▼ Leicester Square is popular with tourists and locals alike. Weekends and evenings see the square filled with revellers.

▲ The White Tower of the Tower of London, one of the top ten tourist attractions in the city, was built by William the Conqueror after he claimed the crown in 1066. It has been used as a royal residence, a barracks, and as a prison. Today it is home to the crown jewels and is open to the public.

▼ River boats like the one shown here take tourists up and down the Thames from central London.

Working in the tourist industry

The number of jobs that overseas tourism provides is even more significant than industry's contribution to the city's wealth. It is estimated that a one per cent increase in overseas tourist numbers results in a 1.28 per cent increase in jobs in London. Domestic visitors are nothing like as valuable – they tend to make shorter visits and spend money less freely. A one per cent increase in tourists from elsewhere in the UK creates only a 0.34 per cent increase in jobs. Increases in tourist numbers create jobs for waiters, tour guides, and hotel workers, but many more people work in spin-off industries. For example:

• Tourism creates jobs in restaurants – 22 per cent of Britain's restaurants are in London.

• Many tourists like to travel in one of London's traditional black cabs – there are 21,000 black cabs registered in Greater London. And of course these cabs must be serviced, filled with fuel and kept clean, all of which provides more work.

• London's theatres are popular with tourists – 30 per cent of tickets are bought by overseas visitors, creating work for theatre staff and actors.

▲ Open-topped tourist buses are a popular way to see the city. The buses the tour companies use are often old London buses that have been modified.

◄ The entrance to the expensive Ritz Hotel in Piccadilly, an up-market area of central London. There are a large number of five star hotels in London, catering to wealthy visitors. Most of the hotels include prestigious restaurants, providing work for large numbers of highly skilled chefs and waiters.

Leisure and sport

Many of the attractions that bring tourists to London – such as museums, art galleries and restaurants – are also popular with local people. London is a relatively 'young' city, in that 47 per cent of the population are between 16 and 44 years old, compared to 40 per cent for the UK as a whole. Younger people tend to use their leisure time in a more active way, and going out in the city is popular.

Many Londoners also spend their leisure time taking part in sports. There are local football and rugby leagues, swimming clubs, cricket contests and many other team sports. People also enjoy more individual activities such as skateboarding, rock climbing, in-line skating, cycle racing and running.

London's successful bid to host the 2012 Olympics has meant that large new sporting facilities will be built on the site of the Games, on Hackney Marshes to the east of the city. The Marshes had been a very large area of unadorned sports grounds used by thousands of people every weekend. Once the Olympic site has been developed there should be world-class sporting facilities available for the local

▲ Skateboarding is popular among the modernist architecture along the south bank of the Thames.

residents to use. The new Wembley Stadium in north-west London will re-open in 2007 after the demolishing of the old building. The UK national government has already proposed making it part of a bid for the 2018 Football World Cup.

◄ Climbing enthusiasts using a manufactured climbing wall in Mile End. There are no large natural climbing areas in the London region.

▼ Football is one of the most popular sports. There are many football pitches throughout the city.

London and its environment

A third of London is made up of green space, so most Londoners are rarely far from a park or garden. But the environment is about more than simply trees, flowers and plants, although these are important. The quality of life for people who live in the city is also linked to the types of buildings they live in and are surrounded by, and to air quality, and noise levels.

▲ London's parks and green areas provide a refuge for the city's wildlife as well as for its people.

Five key issues

The Mayor's office coordinates environmental policies for London. There are five major areas of concern for London's environmental planners:

1) Air quality and pollution
The Congestion Charge is aimed at improving air quality through reducing traffic. London is also pioneering the use of hydrogen and fuel cell power (see p. 53).

2) Ambient noise
Ambient noise is the background noise that people hear, mainly from transport such as car traffic and landing aircraft (a particularly

▶ Reducing the amount of noise in London, for example noise from building work or road repairs, is one of the aims of the city's planners.

acute problem in Hounslow, the area of west London under the Heathrow airport flight path). One of the aims of introducing hydrogen power to London is to reduce ambient noise – hydrogen-powered vehicles are almost silent.

3) Biodiversity

Biodiversity is the range of different animals and plants that live in an area. London is home to over 1,500 species of plants and 300 types of bird, among other animals. In London biodiversity is helped by making sure that wildlife habitats are not lost, and that more open spaces are created. These include London's rivers, allotments, parks and gardens.

4) Energy

Use of fossil fuels such as petrol causes pollution and is unsustainable, as these will one day run out. London therefore needs to use renewable energy sources wherever possible, and to be as energy-efficient as it can. Hydrogen-powered vehicles are almost emission-free, so do not harm the environment. In 2002, the London Hydrogen Partnership was launched, aiming

to help introduce hydrogen power to the city wherever possible. From 2004 to 2006, Transport for London tested three hydrogen-powered buses (see picture on p. 40), with the intention that more should be introduced if the trial was successful. These are a start, but the city needs to do far more in the future if it is to be truly sustainable.

▼ The Mayor's office environmental plan aims to improve the quality of life for all Londoners.

▼ Eco-friendly cars like the one below help to lower carbon emissions, making the city greener, quieter, and a better place to live.

▲ This machine collects surface rubbish on the Thames as the tide flows through it.

5) Waste

The city's inhabitants generate vast mountains of waste every day, which has to be disposed of. 177,000 tonnes of litter are dropped every year, costing £100 million in street cleaning. 44 per cent of Londoners see litter as a priority for improving the quality of London's environment.

In an effort to reduce the amount of waste Londoners generate, they are being encouraged to recycle more. Things are improving: in 2001-2 London's household recycling rate was 9.3 per cent, but this rose to 13.2 per cent in 2003-4. The city still has a long way to go, though: the UK's national average for the same year was 17.7 per cent (and even this was far from the national target figure of 25 per cent).

▶ Over the last 10 years, increasing numbers of Londoners have been taking part in recycling schemes, run by their local councils.

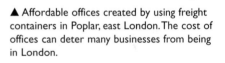

▲ Affordable offices created by using freight containers in Poplar, east London. The cost of offices can deter many businesses from being in London.

Architecture

Many exciting new buildings have been built in London in the last few years, including the Swiss Re Tower (p. 10), Portcullis House (left), the Lloyd's Building (p. 32), and the new City Hall (p. 37). London now has an Architecture and Urbanism Unit, headed by the internationally famous architect Richard Rogers. It aims to create or improve 100 public spaces in the city by 2010, making the physical environment of the city more pleasant for its inhabitants.

◀ Portcullis House, in Westminster, contains the offices of Members of Parliament.

55

The London of tomorrow

What might the London of the future be like? One of the main influences on this will be the Mayor's strategies for the city. These have already begun to have a significant effect on, for example, traffic – which is probably the most visible result of the forward planning. The introduction of the Congestion Charge showed that London, through the Mayor's office, is not afraid to adopt radical solutions to solve its problems.

The London Plan

The city plans to develop as 'an exemplary, sustainable world city', in the words of the Mayor, based on three key elements:
• Strong, diverse long-term economic growth.
• Social inclusion, to give all Londoners the opportunity to share in future success.
• Key improvements in London's environment and use of resources.
The 'London Plan' has been developed by the Mayor's office to meet these criteria. It targets areas such as housing, employment, transport and the environment. One of the key elements is the promise to build 30,000 new homes in London every year for 15 years, half of which are to be affordable for people on lower incomes. In a survey of Londoners in 2004, 52 per cent of people said that one of the worst things about living in the city was the cost of living. A major part of this is the cost of housing – 93 per cent of people think that housing in London is too expensive. More affordable homes would improve the economic situation of many Londoners.

In such a large city it is difficult to please everyone, and every element of the London Plan has had its critics. But the plan has been approved by the national UK government, and is likely to form the basis of London's future development.

▶ Although a diverse city of over seven million people, the city's population have an identity and common cause as Londoners.

▲ London's Thames Flood Barrier is designed to prevent flooding of the city, by regulating the flow of tidal water.

The Thames Flood Barrier

Janine Walker works for the Environment Agency in the Learning Centre at the Thames Flood Barrier. She works with schools and other groups to explain about the risk of flooding to London and the role the barrier plays in preventing it. The barrier was opened in 1984 and has been used many times to prevent flooding in the city. London is especially vulnerable, due to a combination of climate change causing rising sea levels, and a natural sinking of land in London and the south-east corner of England. The Thames Barrier will reach its design specification in the year 2030. Beyond 2030, the level of protection provided by the barrier will decrease slowly due to climate change and rising sea levels. A new project called Project 2100 is now looking to the future, but as Janine says "A new barrier is not the answer, we need to think about the way we use space in the city and about our own behaviour. We teach about recycling, respect for nature and the river. People will need to understand these issues to help London create a more sustainable future."

Glossary

Allotment A small plot of land in an urban setting generally used for growing food crops.

Bond trading The buying and selling of bonds to profit from short-term fluctuations in the market. A bond is a certificate of debt on which the issuer promises to pay the holder interest.

Brownfield site An urban site that could be used for potential redevelopment .

Commonwealth An organisation of over 50 countries most of which were at one time governed by the UK.

Convenience food Food that is pre-prepared, and therefore requires only to be heated up before it can be served.

Direct action An action, such as a strike, boycott or demonstration, which is meant to have a quick effect and influence the government.

Dissolution Dissolving or breaking up something, particularly an organisation.

EU The European Union, an organisation of 25 western and central European countries that acts together on some economic political and social issues.

Economic depression A period of time when unemployment is high and people have little money to spend.

Ethnic Relating to a group of people who have a shared culture and homeland.

Fast food Food that is sold ready to eat and served to the customer soon after it has been ordered. Burgers and pizza are typical examples of fast food.

GDP – Gross Domestic Product. The total value of goods and services produced in a country during one year.

Infrastructure The physical things that a modern country needs to run efficiently, such as roads, railways, airports and power stations.

National Insurance The UK system where everyone pays a proportion of their salary to the government, which in turn provides health care and pensions for citizens.

Nutritious Full of nutrients, chemicals the body needs in order to stay healthy.

Obesity The condition of being so overweight that it is bad for your health.

Plague A fast-spreading disease that affects a large proportion of the population.

Public housing Housing provided by the local government, which is available at a low rent to people who would otherwise find it hard to afford a similar home.

Redevelop To improve a run-down area by repairing its buildings and making better use of any waste ground.

Regeneration Regrowth and recovery: in cities, regenerated areas are those that have undergone redevelopment.

Retail sector The part of the economy to do with selling goods to the general public – shops, in other words, such as clothes, CD or electrical goods stores.

Semi-detached house A house that is joined only to one other.

Suburbs A residential area on the edge of a large town or city.

Sustainability Living in a way that does not spoil the world for future generations, for example making sure that trees that are cut down are replaced, or not acting in a way that will change the world's climate forever.

Urbanisation The process by which a population becomes more concentrated into towns or cities.

Utilities Essential services such as gas, water or electricity supplies.

Wholesale The business of buying and selling goods in large quantities, at a relatively low price. Single items cannot be bought, as in retail.

Further information

Useful websites:

http://ceroi.net/cle/
This site for a City Lifestyle Explorer allows you to discover how your actions as a city dweller have an impact on the city's environment.

The Mayor and the London Assembly are committed to providing information about the city on the Internet, rather than in print, as a way of saving resources. As a result there are some excellent websites dealing with almost every aspect of London life:

www.london.gov.uk
The website of the London Authority, with lots of useful snippets of information about living in London. The section on the Mayor is particularly useful.

www.tfl.gov.uk
Allows you to find out about the congestion charge, London's experiments with hydrogen power, cycling in the city, the tube, buses and many other topics.

www.cityoflondon.gov.uk
Concerned with the Corporation of London and the City, this site is a good source of information about London's economy.

www.visitlondon.com
Concerned mainly with tourism and attractions in London, this site has plenty of useful information and is especially interesting if you've never visited the city.

Books to read:

Horrible Histories: Loathsome London Terry Deary (Scholastic Hippo, 2005)
Full of fascinating facts about the history of London.

Spies, Secret Agents and Spooks of London Natasha Narayan (Watling Street, 2004)
A great romp through some of the more unusual facts and figures of London's history.

Great Plague and Fire – London in Crisis Richard Tames (Heinemann Library, 1999)
This book explains clearly why the Great Fire was such a key event in London's history.

The Great Fire of London Gillian Clements (Franklin Watts, 2002)
A lively look at one of the key events in London's history.

The Story of London: from Roman River to Capital City Jacqui Bailey (A&C Black, 2000)
A very quick whizz through London's key events and historical figures.

Internet-linked Book of London Moira Butterfield and Peter Matthews (Usborne, 2001)
A travel-guide to the city for young people, with Internet links to allow you to get further information.

The Lonely Londoners Sam Selvon (Longman, 1979 but still available)
A much-praised account of what it was like to be a West Indian arriving in London in the 1960s.

London Siege Jim Eldridge (Puffin Books, 2003)
The story of how a soldier acts to save the victims of an embassy siege in London. Packed with facts for the technically minded.

Index